Amazing Ants

Sue Whiting

Contents

Ants Everywhere!

Ants live in nearly every part of the world. These six-legged creatures can be found in hot deserts, steamy tropical jungles, and even where there's snow and ice. Over 10,000 different kinds of ants live all over the world.

An ant guards the ▶
entrance to its nest.

◀ A trail of ants
searches for food
among the leaves
on the forest floor.

Chapter 1

Active Ants

Ants are hardly ever alone. They live and work together in large groups called **colonies**. The **queen** is the most important ant in the colony. Worker ants and male ants called **drones** live in the colony, too.

Ant colonies live in nests. Different kinds of ants build their nests in different places. Some ants build their nests under the ground. Other ants build their nests in small piles of dirt, leaves, or twigs.

Ants need to be able to communicate with each other. They communicate using **scents**, or smells. Ants give off different smells to communicate different messages.

▼ Ants communicate using their sense of smell.

Some ants make nests out of leaves and twigs.

Chapter 2

Inside the Nest

An ant's nest is its home. Just like your home, an ant's nest has different rooms. Ants use the rooms for different things.

The rooms in the nest are called **chambers**. Each chamber has holes to let air in. The queen ant lives in one chamber. Food is stored in some chambers. Other chambers are used as **nurseries** for eggs. Long tunnels join the chambers together.

Nurseries

Queen's chamber

Food chamber

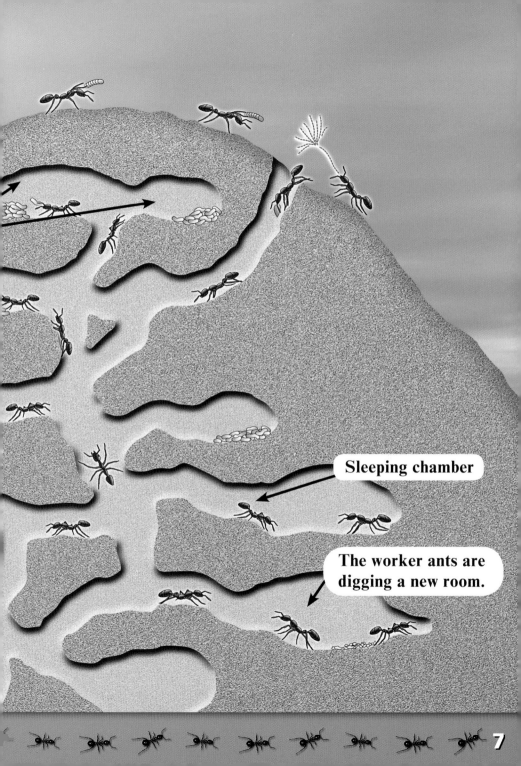

Sleeping chamber

The worker ants are digging a new room.

Chapter 3

Ants at Work

Ants hurry and scurry all over an anthill. What are they doing? The ants are all very busy. These tiny insects are hardworking and well organized. Each ant has a special job. In every colony, ants are divided into three groups: queens, drones, and worker ants. They all work together so that their colony will survive.

▼ Some ants build very large nests.

The Queen

How would you like to lie around all day with your every need taken care of? Well, that's the life the queen ant enjoys. There is usually only one queen in each colony. She is the largest ant in the colony. Her job is to lay eggs.

▲ The queen ant is the biggest ant in the colony.

When a queen ant is born, she has wings. The newly hatched queen ant flies away from the nest to look for a mate. When she is ready to lay her eggs, the queen looks for a good place for a nest. Then she breaks off her wings and digs a small tunnel. She lays her eggs inside the tunnel, starting a new colony.

A queen ant is the only ant that lays eggs. ▶

Worker Ants

The ants you see around the garden or in your house are the worker ants. They are smaller than the queen. They don't have wings. Worker ants are always female, but they can't lay eggs.

Worker ants are the busiest of all the ants. They do all the work for the colony. Luckily, there are thousands of worker ants in each colony.

Some worker ants feed the colony. They gather food and bring it back to the nest. Worker ants can carry loads that are more than ten times their own weight.

Some worker ants look after the queen. Their job is to feed her and keep her safe. Other worker ants take care of the nest. They keep it clean and build new chambers and tunnels.

Worker ants clean the queen.

▲ A worker ant gathers food for the colony.

▲ Worker ants take care of the cocoons.

Some worker ants are like nurses. They look after the eggs. They lick them to keep them clean. Soon **larvae** hatch out of the eggs. The larvae look like tiny white worms, but they are baby ants. They don't have legs and they don't move around much on their own. Worker ants spit up food to feed the larvae. Then the larvae spin **cocoons** around themselves. Inside the cocoons, the larvae will change into adult ants.

Drones

Male ants are called drones. When they hatch out of their cocoons, drones are bigger than worker ants. They also have wings. Drones, like queens, have only one job to do. That job is to mate with the new queen. After mating, the male ants die. But new ant colonies are born.

▼ Male ants fly from the nest to find mates.

Chapter 4

Amazing Ants

There are more than 10,000 different kinds of ants around the world. Not all ants live in the same kind of nests or eat the same food. But all ants live in colonies. Some of the more unusual colonies are really amazing.

Carpenter Ants

Carpenter ants make their nests in wood. They dig into the wood to carve out tunnels and chambers. These ants don't eat the wood. They carry it back outside the nest. The walls inside the nest are clean and smooth.

Most of the time carpenter ants make their nests in trees and logs. Sometimes carpenter ants find their way into houses. They like damp places like kitchens and bathrooms. Carpenter ants can do a lot of damage to a house. The wooden floors and doorways of houses can be destroyed.

◄ Carpenter ants make their nest in wood.

▼ Carpenter ants have damaged the door-way of this house.

Carpenter ants have made tunnels and a nest inside this doorway.

The ants carried the wood out of the doorway to make room for their nest.

Leaf-Cutter Ants

Leaf-cutter ants are farmers. They farm **fungus**, which is like the mold that you see on an old piece of bread or fruit. Leaf-cutter ants feed their colonies with the fungus they grow.

Leaf-cutter ants are mostly found in hot, steamy parts of Central and South America. The ants leave the nest in search of juicy, green leaves. They use their sharp saw-toothed jaws to slice the leaves into small pieces. Sometimes leaf-cutter ants cut all of the leaves from a tree!

▼ Leaf-cutter ants carry leaves back to the nest.

Once the leaf is cut, the leaf-cutter ants lift it overhead and take it back to the nest. The ants look like they are carrying little green umbrellas.

Inside the nest, other ants work like gardeners. They lick the leaves clean. Then the ants chew the leaves into a squishy **pulp**. The pulp is poked into the chamber that is the fungus garden. Fungus grows quickly on the leaf pulp. The fungus is the food for the ant colony.

▲ Leaf-cutter ants have sharp teeth.

Army Ants

Army ants march through the jungles of South America and Africa. Unlike other types of ants, army ants travel long distances to find food. The ants move in long, thick columns as they march through the jungle.

An army ant colony can travel over large areas of jungle in a day. The ants will eat any small creature in their path. They can eat a mouse in a few minutes. Army ants will even attack larger animals like pigs and goats.

Army ants make unusual nests. They don't dig or build nests like other ants. Their nest is made out of army ants! They cling to each other and make walls and tunnels and chambers. They surround the queen, her eggs, and the larvae. When the larvae are ready to hatch, the nest breaks up. The colony is on the move again!

Army ants eat ▶
any small animal
in their path.

Army ants march
in a column
through the jungle.

Honeypot Ants

Honeypot ants are found in dry, warm areas of the world, including parts of the United States, Africa, and Australia. Honeypot ants have found an amazing way to store food. Special worker ants store food in their stomachs. These worker ants are called **repletes**, which means they are full of food.

▼ This honeypot ant's stomach is full of food.

▲ Repletes hang in a chamber.

Worker ants collect food for the repletes to eat.
The repletes' stomachs become very large and round
because they eat so much. They become so full and heavy
that they can't move. The repletes hang from
the walls of chambers deep in the nest. When other
sources of food are scarce, the other ants rub the
repletes. This causes the repletes to spit up drops
of food for the other ants to eat.

Ants are some of the most organized creatures in the insect world. Each ant has a special job to do. Whether a queen, a drone, or a worker ant, each ant is important. By working together they can build a nest and help the colony grow.

▼ What ants can you find where you live?

chamber   a room inside an ant's nest

cocoon   a silky covering that an ant larva spins around itself

colony   a large group of ants that live and work together

drone   a male ant

fungus   a kind of mold

larva   a worm-like baby that hatches out of an ant egg

nursery   the area in the nest where the eggs are cared for

pulp   chewed-up and squishy leaves

queen   the largest ant in a colony and the only ant that lays eggs

replete   a kind of honeypot worker ant that stores food in its stomach

scent   the smell given off by ants to pass on messages to other ants

Index